Linux CLI Pocket Book

Linux CLI Pocket Book
Dustin Davis

TABLE OF CONTENTS

Navigation and Fundamentals

Navigation

Command	Notes
cd <directory>	Navigate to the specified directory, i.e. cd /var/log
cd ~	Navigate to current user's home directory
cd ..	Navigate up one directory
cd -	Navigate to the previous directory you were in
pushd <directory>	Pushes the specified directory to memory
popd	Navigate to the last directory pushed to memory
ls	List the contents of the current directory
ls -lahS <directory>	List the contents of /var/log in long format, including hidden files, with human-readable sizes, sorted by size
ls -lt <directory>	List the contents of /var/log in long format, sorted by time last modified
ls -R	Recursively list subdirectories in the current directory
\ls	Execute ls without its associated alias. Useful when you don't want linux to touch the metadata of files in large queries
pwd	Prints the current directory

File and Directory Operations

Command	Notes
rm <file>	Removes / deletes a file
rm -rf <directory>	Removes a directory and all of its contents
mkdir </path/to/directory>	Create a new directory at specified location
cp <file> </new/location>	Copies a file to a new location
cp -p <file> </new/location>	Copies file to new location while preserving the permissions of the original
mv <file> </new/location/>	Moves a file to a specified new location
file <filename>	Get info on the file type

Command	Notes
cat <filename>	Print contents of file to terminal
gzcat <filename.gz>	Print contents of a gzipped file to terminal
less <filename>	Scroll through contents of a file one line at a time
tail -n 100 <filename>	Print the last 100 lines of a file to terminal
tail -f <filename>	Follow the contents of a file, printing new content to the terminal as it is written to file

Basic System Operations

Command	Notes
w	View basic system info, including uptime, logged in users, and CPU load average
id <username>	Print user and group info. Leave username blank to view current user
whoami	Print the current user
shutdown now	Shutdown the system immediately
shutdown +5	Shutdown the system in 5 minutes
reboot now	Reboot the system immediately
history	View users shell history
!300	Execute the command found at line 300 in the users shell history
man <command>	Display the manual for the specified command
which <command>	Print the location of a command's executable

Important Locations

Command	Notes
/etc/fstab	Mount configurations
/etc/crypttab	Encrypted block device configuration
/etc/hosts	Address translation
/etc/crontab	Scheduled jobs
/etc/hosts	Associates names with IP addresses
/etc/hosts.allow	Allowed network ACLs
/etc/hosts.deny	Denied network ACLs
/etc/hostname	System hostname
/dev/null	Blackhole. Redirect output here to discard it
/etc/passwd	Information on system accounts
/etc/shadow	System account password hashes/information
/var/log	Log directory
/etc/resolv.conf	DNS resolver configuration
/dev	Device files
/etc/issue	Contains the message printed at the login prompt
/proc/cpuinfo	CPU information
/proc/filesystems	Filesystem information
/etc/systemd	Local systemD configurations
/usr/lib/systemd/system	Unit files of installed packages
/etc/logrotate.d	Logrotate configurations

Compression / Decompression

Command	Notes
tar -cvf my_archive.tar /tmp/mydir	Archive the directory "/tmp/mydir" as "my_archive.tar"
tar -tf my_archive.tar	Displays archive contents
tar -cvzf my_archive.tar.gz /tmp/mydir	Archives and compresses the directory using gzip
tar -xvf my_archive.tar	Extracts my_archive.tar
tar -xzvf my_archive.tar.gz	Decompress and extract my_archive.tar.gz
tar -xzvf my_archive.tar.gz --strip 1	Strips first item of archive when extracting. Useful when you want to remove the parent directory

Redirection

Command	Notes
<command> 2>errors.txt	Redirects STDERR to the file "errors.txt"
<command> > myFile.txt	Redirects STDOUT to myFile.txt and overwrites its contents
<command> >> myFile.txt	Redirects STDOUT to myFlle.txt and appends to the end of the file
<command> > /dev/null 2>&1	Redirect both STDOUT and STDERR to /dev/null, discarding both

Permissions

sudo

Command	Notes
sudo <command>	Perform a command as the superuser
sudo su -	Enter a shell within root's environment
sudo !!	Perform the previous command as a super user
sudo -l -U <user>	Check a user's effective sudo permissions
sudo -u <user> test -r <file>; echo$?	Test if the specified user has read access to the file, 0 = yes, 1 = no
sudo -u <user> test -w <file>; echo$?	Test if the specified user has write access to the file, 0 = yes, 1 = no
visudo	Open the sudoers file with vi. Always use this command to make edits, never manually edit the file.

Grant full sudo permissions to a specific group

```
cat > /etc/sudoers.d/it-team << "EOF"
%it-team ALL=(ALL) ALL
EOF

# Always change the permissions so it can't be modified
chmod 440 /etc/sudoers.d/it-team
```

Grant sudo permissions to a group for a specific subset of commands.

```
cat > /etc/sudoers.d/devops-team << "EOF"
Cmnd_Alias APACHE_CMDS = /bin/systemctl start httpd, /bin/systemctl restart httpd, /bin/systemctl stop httpd
%devops-team ALL=(ALL) APACHE_CMDS
EOF
chmod 440 /etc/sudoers.d/devops-team
```

File Permissions

Command	Notes
chown <user>:<group> <file/directory>	Changes the owner (user and group) of the specified file or directory
chmod gu+wrx <file>	Gives the user owner and group owner of the file: write, read, and execute permissions

Command	Notes
chmod o-w <file>	Removes write permissions from "other" users (not the user or group owner)
chmod 777 <file>	Gives read, write, and execute permissions to all users, using numeric permissions
getfacl <file>	Print FACL (File Access Control List) for specified file
setfacl -m u:bob:rw /tmp/data	Grants user "bob" read and write permissions to /tmp/data
setfacl -m g:marketing:rwx /tmp/marketing	Grants group "marketing" read, write, and execute permissions to /tmp/marketing
setfacl -R -m u:bob:rwx /tmp/data	Grants 'bob' user read/write/execute permissions to /tmp/data and ALL files/folders within it (recursively)
setfacl -x u:bob /tmp/data	Removes permissions from /tmp/data for user "bob"
setfacl -b /tmp/data	Removes all ACLs from /tmp/data

Understanding Numeric Permissions

Numeric Notation	File Permission
0	---
1	--x
2	-w-
3	-wx
4	r--
5	r-x
6	rw-
7	rwx

SELinux

Command	Notes
getenforce	Print the current mode of SELinux
sestatus	Print current status of SELinux
cat /var/log/messages | grep -i selinux **OR** cat /var/log/audit/audit.log | grep -i selinux	Search logs for SELinux events
journalctl -t setroubleshoot	View journal entries for SELinux
ausearch -m AVC,USER_AVC -ts recent	View recent SELinux denials
semanage boolean -l	List SELinux booleans and their current and default settings
setsebool <boolean> on	Set a specified SELinux boolean to "on"
ls -lZ <file>	Print the security contexts of a file
restorecon <file>	Restores a file's default SELinux security contexts

Package Management

YUM

Command	Notes
yum -y install <package>	Install package and accept all prompts automatically
yum search <package>	Search for a package
yum list <package> --showduplicates	List all available versions of a package
yum info <package>	Retrieve info about a package
yum list installed	List all installed packages
yum deplist <package>	List all dependencies of a package
yum remove <package>	Uninstall a package
yum autoremove <package>	Uninstall a package and all dependencies
yum clean all	Clean yum cache
yum update	Update packages
yum history info <package>	List history of installation/upgrades of a specific package
yum downgrade <old_package>	Downgrade a package to a previous version

RPM

Command	Notes
rpm -qc <package>	List configuration files of a package
rpm -qa <package>	Check if you have a package installed
rpm -ql <package>	List what the package will install
rpm -qR <package>	List package dependencies
rpm -qi <package>	Get package info
rpm --test -i <package>	Performs a dry-run of an install of the package

14

APT

Command	Notes
apt-get install <package>	Installs a package
apt-get update	Updates source list to ensure you get the most up-to-date packages
apt-get upgrade	Upgrades all installed packages to most recent version
apt-get autoclean	Cleanup unneeded package files
apt-get clean	Cleans APT cache
apt-get check	Checks for problems and broken dependencies
apt-get remove <package>	Remove a package without touching the configuration files
apt-get purge <package>	Removes a package and all configuration files
apt-get autoremove <package>	Remove a package and all dependencies

DPKG

Command	Notes
dpkg -l	List installed packages
dpkg -s <package>	Check if a package is installed
dpkg -L <package>	List location of installed package
cat /var/lib/dpkg/info/<package>.conffiles	List configuration files for an installed package

15

Services

SystemD

Command	Notes
systemctl status <service>	Check the current status of a service
systemctl start <service>	Start a service
systemctl stop <service>	Stop a service
systemctl restart <service>	Restart a service
systemctl list-unit-files –t service	List all services that are registered in systemd
systemctl list-unit-files –t service | grep -i http	Search for a specific service using grep
systemctl enable <service>	Tell service to start upon boot
systemctl disable <service>	Tell service not to start upon boot
systemctl mask <service>	Link service to /dev/null so it cannot be started
systemctl daemon-reload	Reloads any changes or additions of unit files

service

Command	Notes
service —status-all	List the status of all services
service <service> status	Check status of a service
service <service> start	Start a service
service <service> stop	Stop a service
service <service> restart	Restart a service
/etc/init.d/	Location of scripts used by the 'service' command

JournalD

Command	Notes
vim /etc/systemd/journal.conf	Edit the journalD configuration file
journalctl -u <service>	View journal for the specified service. You can also provide a user or unit instead of a service
journalctl -xe -u <service>	Jump to the end of the journal for a specified service, with extra catalog info included
echo "hello" | systemd-cat	Sends STDOUT (in this case, "hello") to the journal
journalctl —vacuum-time=3d	Delete everything but the last 2 days of journal entries
journalctl —vacuum-size=750M	Delete everything but the most recent 750MB of journal entries
	Other Useful "journalctl" Flags:
-r	Show the newest entries at the top
-n 100	Only show the 100 most recent entries
-f	Follow entries as they are written
-b	Only show entries since the last system boot
—since / —until	Specify a time window
—disk-usage	Check how much disk space the journal is using
—rotate	Rotate journal files

Storage and Filesystems

Querying Storage Information

Command	Notes
df –h	List disk statistics with human readable sizes
df –i	List disk inode statistics
df -T	List disks and their filesystem type
lsblk	List block devices
blkid	List block device attributes
pvdisplay	Print physical devices
vgdisplay	Print volume groups
lvdisplay	Print logical volumes
ls –la /dev/disk/by-uuid	List disks and their respective UUIDs

Mounts

Command	Notes
mount	List all mounts
mount -a	Mount everything found in /etc/fstab
mount /dev/sdb2 /mnt/myMount	Mounts the /dev/sdb2 filesystem to directory /mnt/my-Mount
mount -t <type> <filesystem> <mountpoint>	Mount a filesystem with specific type, i.e. CIFS
umount -l /mnt/myMount	Lazy unmount, waits until the filesystem is no longer busy before unmounting it
umount -f /mnt/myMount	Forced unmount, immediately unmounts the filesystem. Use with caution.
vim /etc/fstab	Edit mount configuration file. Mounts configured here will be mounted upon system boot
echo 7 > /proc/fs/cifs/cifsFYI	Enable more verbose CIFs debugging. Remember to echo 1 when you are finished

Troubleshooting Disk Usage

Command	Notes
du -sh /var/log/* | sort -h	Print the grand total size each file and folder in /var/log, and sort by size
du -sh /var/log/* —exclude="dmesg*"	Print the grand total size of everything in /var/log EXCEPT for files that start with "dmesg"
find /var/log/nginx -maxdepth 1 -mindepth 1 -type f -mtime +30 -exec rm -rf {} \;	Delete files in /var/log/nginx which are older than 30 days
find /var/log/nginx -maxdepth 1 -mindepth 1 -type f -mtime +7 -name "access*" -exec rm -rf {} \;	Delete files in /var/log/nginx which are older than 7 days and name begins with "access"
fsck -A <partition>	Check all filesystems on partition for errors. Ensure partition is not mounted before running.

Networking

FirewallD

Command	Notes
firewall-cmd --list-all	List all zones and rules
firewall-cmd --zone=<zone> --list-all	List all rules for a specific zone
firewall-cmd --permanent --zone=public --add-source=192.168.10.0/24	Allow traffic originating from the 'source' subnet through the firewall under the public zone
firewall-cmd --reload	Reload any '--permanent' changes, so they persist through firewall or system restart
firewall-cmd --permanent --zone=public --add-port=80/tcp	Allow traffic through port 80
firewall-cmd --permanent --zone=public --add-rich-rule='rule family="ipv4" source address="192.168.10.12" port port="161" protocol="udp" accept'	Allows: - ipv4 traffic - originating from 192.168.10.12 - on port 161 - using udp
firewall-cmd --permanent --zone=public --add-forward-port=port=80:proto=tcp:toaddr=192.168.10.12	Forwards incoming traffic on port 80 to the host at 192.168.10.12
firewall-cmd --permanent --zone=home --change-interface=ens192	Move network interface "ens192" to the home zone
firewall-cmd --permanent --zone=public --add-service=ssh	Allow service "ssh" through the firewall under the public zone

Troubleshooting

Command	Notes
sudo lsof -nPi TCP	List ports that services have established connections on or are listening on
sudo watch -n 2 ss -antp	Monitor listening and established connections, refreshed every 2 seconds
ping <host>	Ping a host to check connectivity. Provide either an IP address or hostname
nslookup <target>	DNS lookup
dig @8.8.8.8 <target>	DNS lookup, using 8.8.8.8 as the name server
traceroute <host>	Trace network route to host

Command	Notes
tcpdump	Packet capture, see the tcpdump section of this book
nc <address> <port>	Make raw TCP connection to an address and port. Useful for determining if a host is accepting connections on a specific port.
nc -l -p <port>	Listen for connections on specified port
arp	Print ARP table

Network Configuration

Command	Notes
ip addr	List network interfaces
ifconfig	List network interfaces (legacy)
ip route	List network routes
systemctl restart networking	Restart networking service
ifdown <interface> && ifup <interface>	Bring an interface down and immediately bring it back up
/etc/sysconfig/network-scripts/ifcfg-*	Location of network interface config files (RHEL/CentOS)
/etc/network/interfaces	Location of network interface configurations (Debian)

Common Ports

Port	Notes
21	FTP
22	SSH
23	Telnet
25	SMTP
53	DNS
67/68	DHCP
69	TFTP
80	HTTP
88	Kerberos
110	POP3
123	NTP
143	IMAP
161	SNMP
201	AppleTalk
389	LDAP
443	HTTPS
546/547	DHCPv6
902	VMWare
2049	NFS
3306	MySQL
3389	RDP

TCPDUMP

TCPDUMP

Command	Notes
tcpdump -i ens192 port 80	Capture traffic on interface "ens192" over port 80
tcpdump -D	List all available interfaces to listen on
tcpdump -i any icmp	Capture on any interface for icmp packets
tcpdump -i <interface> host 192.168.10.12	Capture on a specific interface for any traffic to or from a specific host
tcpdump -i <interface> src 192.168.10.12 port 80	Capture for traffic on port 80 originating from a specific host
tcpdump -i <interface> "port 80 and (dst 192.168.10.12 or dst 192.168.10.13)"	Capture for traffic on port 80 destined for either specified address

Useful TCPDUMP Flags

Flag	Notes
-nn	Disable port and address name resolution
-A	Print packet contents in ASCII
-x	Print packet contents in hex
-c100	Capture 100 packets then stop listening
-w <file_name>	Save packet capture to a .pcap file instead of printing them to STDOUT
-v / -vv / -vvv	Verbose output, additional 'v's means more verbosity
-r <file_name>	Read the packets from a .pcap file

Understanding Packet Flags

Flag	Notes
S	SYN (Synchronisation)
.	ACK (Acknowledgement)
F	FIN (Finish)
R	RST (Reset)
P	PSH (Push)
U	URG (Urgent)

Processes

Processes

Command	Notes
ps aux	List all running processes and their owners
kill <pid>	Kill the process with the specified PID
kill -9 <pid>	Send the "SIGKILL" signal instead of the default SIGTERM to PID
kill -l	List available kill signals
pkill httpd	Kill process "httpd"
pkill -t pts/1	Kill all open processes under a specific terminal
top	View up-to-date and sorted process information

PGREP

Command	Notes
pgrep <name> -l	greps for a process and prints the PID and process name
pgrep -u <user> -l	Prints PID and process name for processes running under a specific user
pgrep -u john -l python	Shows python processes running under user "john"

Remote Operations

WGET / CURL

Command	Notes
wget http://192.168.10.12/files/some_file.tar.gz	Downloads a remote file over http
wget -O compressed_file.tar.gz <remote_file>	Downloads a remote file over http and saves it as "compressed_file.tar.gz"
curl -s https://www.google.com/	Invoke GET method for google.com silently (without progress bar)

curl -X PUT <URL> -H 'Content-Type: application/json' -d'
{
  "foo": {
    "bar": {}
  }
}
'
	Invoke PUT method with specified header and data

SCP (Secure Copy)

Command	Notes
scp <username>@<remote_host>:<file_location> <local_directory>	Downloads a file from a remote host to the local system
scp foo.txt john@host2:/home/john	Sends foo.txt on the local system to /home/john on remote host "host2"
scp -r <local_directory> <username>@<remote_host>:<remote_directory>	Sends an entire directory from the local host to a remote host

SSH (Secure Shell) and Telnet

Command	Notes
ssh <user>@<host>	Login to a host with specified user
ssh <user>@<host> -p <port>	Login to a host on a non-standard port
ssh-keygen	Generate key pair on local system
ssh-copy-id <user>@<host>	Copy public key to remote system
telnet <host> <port>	Telnet to host on specific port. Remember, unlike SSH, telnet is not secure

GREP / AWK / SED

GREP

Command	Notes
ls /var/log | grep -i log	List contents of /var/log containing the case-insensitive string "log"
grep -i error /var/log/messages	Print every line of the file /var/log/messages which contains the case-insensitive string "error"
grep -i error -r /var/log/	Recursively search all files and directories in /var/log, and print lines which contain the case-insensitive string "error"
cat /var/log/messages | grep -iv error	Prints every line in /var/log/messages which does not contain the case-insensitive string "error"
ip addr show eth0 | egrep -o "\b([0-9]{1,3}\.){3}[0-9]{1,3}\b"	Pipe output of a command to grep and print the results of the regular expression, in this case, searching for IP addresses

AWK

Command	Notes
awk '{print $1 "\t" $3}' <file>	Prints fields 1 and 3 from specified file, separated by a tab
awk –F : '{print $1 "\t" $3}' <file>	Changes the delimiter to a colon instead of the default space/tab
awk '/<regular_expression>/' <file>	Print lines matching the regular expression
cat <file> | awk '$1 !~ /error/ { print $2 }'	Pipe output of a command to awk, then print the second field, but only when the first field does not contain "error"

SED

Command	Notes
sed -i '/<regular_expression>/d' <file>	Delete all lines in the file which match the regular expression
sed -i'.old' '/<regular_expression>/d' <file>	Same as above, but saves a backup of the original file with ".old" appended to the filename
sed -i 's/192.168.1.115/10.0.1.115/g' <file>	Replaces all instances of IP address 192.168.0.115 with 10.0.1.115 in the specified file.
sed 's/192.168.1.115/10.0.1.115/g' <original_file> > <new_file>	Same as above, except instead of editing the original file in place, write the changes to a new file
w | sed '1,2d'	Print the results of the 'w' command with the first two lines deleted

SCREEN

Screen

Command	Notes
screen	Open a new screen session
screen -S <name>	Open a new screen session with a specific name
screen -ls	List all screen sessions
screen -r <name>	Resume screen session
	Screen Interactions (for example: "ctrl+a c" means press ctrl+a at once, then press c)
ctrl+a c	Create new window
ctrl+a A	Rename window
ctrl+a d	Detach from current session
ctrl+a "	List all sessions
ctrl+a S	Split current session horizontally into a new session
ctrl+a |	Split current session vertically into a new session
ctrl+a ' <name>	Switch to specific session
ctrl+a Q	Remove all sessions except current session
ctrl+a X	Remove current session
ctrl+a k	Kill current session

VIM

Insert Mode Controls

Keystroke	Notes
i	Insert mode, for editing the file
a	Insert mode, but cursor jumps to the end of the current character
o	Insert mode, but below the current line
Escape Key	Escape insert mode

Navigation

Keystroke	Notes
w	Move to beginning of next word
b	Move to beginning of previous word
e	Move to the end of current word
0	Move to the beginning of the line
$	Move to the end of the line
%	Jumps to the matching { (' " < [pair character

Editor Controls

Keystroke	Notes
u	Undo
.	Redo last block of entries
>>	Insert an indent
<<	Remove indent
v	Visual mode, use arrow keys to select text

Keystroke	Notes
shift + v	Block visual mode, use arrow keys to select a block of text
y	Copy selection
p	Paste below
P	Paste above
d	Delete current character
dd	Delete current line
de	Delete to end of word
r <character>	Replaces the current character with a new one
/	Search for text. Hit enter, press 'n' for next result
dG	Delete current and all following lines

Commands

Command	Notes
:q!	Quit without saving
:w	Save
:x	Save and quit
:saveas <name>	Save as a new file
:f	Get info on currently open file
:%s/ip/IP/gc	Replaces all instances of "ip" with "IP". Optional 'c' character requests confirmation before replacing each instance.
:!<command>	Runs a command outside of vim
:r!pwd	Executed 'pwd' command and inserts the results into the file
:set paste	Enters paste mode. Pasting contents of your clipboard will now be parsed with vim's settings.
:set number	Show line numbers

Command	Notes
:bad <file>	Adds a file to the buffer (for working with multiple files).
:bn	Jump to the next file in the buffer
:history	Show your command history

Miscellaneous Useful Commands

Useful Commands

Command	Notes
echo $?	Prints the return code of the previous command
watch -n5 -c"<command>"	Print results of the specified command, refreshed every 5 seconds
uname -a	Print system information
dmesg -T | tail -n 100	Print the last 100 lines of the kernel logs with human readable timestamps
datetimectl	View or modify date and time settings
hostnamectl	View or modify hostname settings
python -c "<python_code>"	Execute a one-off python command
alias	List all aliases
ctrl+r <search_term>	Type to search for previous commands
ctrl+c	Interrupt program execute, halting immediately
clear	Clears the terminal window
cat <file> | cut -d : -f 1	For each line of a file, print everything before the first colon

NOTES

NOTES

NOTES

NOTES